Playing with Rainbows
Jane Gray

Playing with Rainbows

Jane Gray

Ellingham Press

First published 2011
©Jane Gray 2011
British Library Cataloguing-in-Publication Data
A catalogue record for this book is available from the British Library
ISBN 978-0-9563079-3-4

Cover design by Goosey Graphics www.gooseygraphics.co.uk
Typesetting and design by eMC Design www.emcdesign.org.uk
Printed and bound in the UK by MPG Books Group, Bodmin and King's Lynn

Published by Ellingham Press, 43 High Street, Much Wenlock, Shropshire TF13 6AD
www.ellinghampress.co.uk

Foreword

When Jane Ross (as she then was) applied to the Royal College of Art to study stained glass, I had no hesitation in accepting her as a student, and when she had completed her studies the quality of her work led me to offer her the job as my assistant for the Coventry windows.

There followed a very fruitful working relationship which grew closer over time, and matured into a lasting friendship. And when she married Kiril (or Mr Jane Gray as he sometimes called himself) I didn't lose an assistant, I gained another firm friend.

I encouraged all my assistants to pursue their own artistic careers and Jane had the necessary courage to do this at a time when it was still an unusual role for a woman. Consequently, I was particularly delighted when she became the first woman to become a liveryman of the Worshipful Company of Glaziers.

Over the years our friendship and ongoing conversations about art and life endured the increasing distance between us as we both moved to different parts of the country, and I watched her career go from strength to strength – her striking colour and design sense finding a ready supply of commissions. So it was a special pleasure to welcome her to my 100th birthday last year.

Her book is a valuable record of what I believe to be a crucial period in stained glass history (in this country at least) as the dead hand of the Victorians finally gave way to a modern aesthetic which still drew much of its inspiration from the greatness of the mediaeval glaziers.

Lawrence Lee

September 2010

Dedication

For my husband Kiril and my daughters Joanna and Sarah

Playing with Rainbows

Introduction

Is it art or craft? Religious or secular? Figurative or abstract?

The answer to the first question 'Art or craft?' is that stained glass is both *art* and *craft*. The answer to the other questions is this – stained glass can be used almost anywhere, in many contexts or situations.

I have tried to show what stained glass has meant to me, and how, using the traditional techniques which I will explain later, I have endeavoured to create windows and panels suitable for varying locations. Rather than any sort of historical account of this medium, I am offering something of a journey through my life and career as a stained glass artist and craftsman.

This little mermaid of Zennor is part of the piece I designed
and made for my National Diploma of Design.

How it all began

It all started when I chose to follow Art for my as-yet-undefined future.

In 1949, I enrolled as a student at Kingston School of Art in Surrey where, for two years, I worked harder than at any other time in my life, before passing the Intermediate Exam, which tested me on my knowledge of anatomy, architecture, drawing, design, colour, sculpture, weaving and lettering. This was the Foundation course, and it was the first step towards the teaching qualification, the National Diploma of Design (NDD). The next step involved a decision to specialize for two more years in a single subject to achieve the NDD. How could I choose?

One of the tutors advised me to visit every department in the Art School before making up my mind. During those first two years I never had time to visit the annexe, and wasn't quite sure what went on there. It was a bit of a walk from the main building, and looked, from the outside, like any ordinary terraced town house, overlooking Kingston bus station. Up the stone steps to the front door, then up uncarpeted stairs towards the sound of glass cutting. So this was where the Stained Glass Department was!

What a revelation. It was love at first sight. Although I don't remember seeing any completed panels I do recall a strong feeling of 'this is what I would like to do'. There were students cutting glass on a bench; others working at easels set up in the window so that light could pass through the coloured glass which they had cut and now were painting; others working at another bench making up panels using strips of lead to hold pieces of glass together, and there were other activities which I couldn't appreciate at first glance.

There is something magical in the way that stained glass only comes to life when light passes through it. The skills needed to create a window include those of drawing and painting, patient attention to detail, a requirement for strong design, and appreciation of how colour is transformed by light. All these things I was aware of and I felt confident that I could enjoy working in this beautiful and fascinating medium. I didn't need to visit any other department. This is what I wanted to do, I told my tutor.

'Stained glass, eh? Not much of a future in that. All the war damage claims will have been completed by now.' (The year was 1950.) 'Besides,' he continued, 'stained glass isn't classified as a main subject of the NDD. You'd have to take a second subject to go with it.' In a sort of double-take, I realized that in his mind stained glass was automatically equated with churches, saints and haloes and all that stuff, whereas in my mind it was colour, shapes, luminosity, playing with rainbows...

'Yes,' I said, 'yes, I'll take a second subject – weaving.' I had done a bit of weaving as part of my Intermediate course, and it seemed to me that laying one coloured thread over another to create a third had a distinct similarity to stained glass. I duly passed my NDD in these two subjects and felt ready to go out and face the world, with letters after my name. I had been a student for four years.

'Just a minute,' said my tutor. 'Think about this: you leave, you apply for a teaching job but the competition will be fierce. There will be others with higher qualifications. If you would be prepared to go on for another three years at the Royal College of Art you will end up with ARCA (Associate of the Royal College of Art) after your name and that, I can assure you, will get you the highest rate of pay among art teachers. And,' he actually wagged his finger at me, 'if you get married and have children and by some stroke of fate you

are widowed, you'll be glad you stayed on for those three years. If, that is, they accept you.' I duly sent in my portfolio and was accepted.

Looking back on it now, for me that first year at the Royal College was somewhat fraught. At Kingston the tutors had cared. They had cared about your work. They cared if you were in some difficulty and they cared if you were, or weren't, there. But at the Royal College of Art you signed the register, then you could go off for the day: visiting the Victoria and Albert (V&A) museum just along the Cromwell Road – or back to bed if you felt so inclined, when there wasn't a compulsory lecture. There were in fact a number of these but to me the freedom of choice on the days without a class or a lecture to attend was almost too much. I became very depressed, and more so because the other students in my year were producing work in large and abstract styles very different from mine. I spoke to the head of department, Lawrence Lee, who appreciated my feelings of inadequacy and general lack of direction. He arranged for me to spend one day a week in the Jewellery Department, which was a delightful experience, and my spirits were lifted. Jewellery has always seemed to me like a miniature form of stained glass. Incidentally, I am still wearing the earrings, bracelet and rings which I made on those Fridays.

During their second year, students had the compulsory task of making a copy of an actual panel of stained glass which could be chosen from those housed in the V&A museum. The gallery devoted to stained glass was being reorganized just then, and I was able, literally, to get my hands on a small Flemish fifteenth-century tracery light and with tender loving care I worked on copying this little panel which taught me more about glass painting than anything or anybody else ever has.

Copying this small 15th-century Flemish window taught me more about stained glass than anyone or anything else has ever done.

Making a window

Here perhaps I should say something about how a window is made. Most people know that a stained glass window is made from pieces of coloured glass held together by strips of lead with an H section (the H lying on its side), which enclose the pieces of glass and separate them one from another – and also that stained glass can only be viewed successfully if there is a source of light *behind* it. The aim of the designer is *to control* the amount of light coming through the glass so that the viewer looks *at* the window rather than *through* it.

Before making a window there has to be the need for a window. This may come in the form of a memorial; a public celebration of some special event; an anniversary; a screen to block out an unwelcome view, or simply the need to have some beautiful illuminating colour enhancing a space. Whatever and wherever it is needed, it has to be designed.

Having been brought up using imperial measurements I work at a scale of one inch to the foot. The average proportions of a single light window in a parish church are approximately 6 feet high by 18 inches wide, so that my design would measure 6 inches by 1½ inches on the page. Assuming that I have received a commission to design a memorial window of this proportion I start by doing necessary research, i.e. learning about the deceased; their interests, commitments, love of colours/music/hobbies, etc; after which I have to face that awful expanse of white paper on my drawing board and START DRAWING…never easy.

This is my design for the nativity window in St John's Episcopal Church in Perth which I made in 1964.

After some hours, hopefully, there will be something to see…Then comes the long and arduous time when the ideas and shapes come together – the lead lines are drawn in, the divisions are established, the colours are chosen and applied, the tone values are corrected, and, at last, the design is mounted on a suitably coloured card, the description is typed, and the creation is sent to the client.

Now comes the waiting. The design has to be seen and approved by the client first of all, then the Parochial Church Council (PCC) has to display the artwork to allow the congregation to approve it. After that, it has to go before the Diocesan Advisory Committee (DAC). This body has to include architects, historians and/or people who have knowledge of the church and its traditions and who are aware of what is either suitable or unsuitable in a window. If the design is successful it has to have a Faculty granted, which is a legal approval. Only at this point does the design come back to me. These procedures may take several months as the PCC and DAC do not meet very often.

I now have to enlarge my design up to its full size. This can be done by hand, but I prefer to have it done photographically. This is costly, but it saves many hours of concentrated work. After receiving the enlargement I lay it on a large flat surface and, using detail paper (a type of tracing paper), I trace through the lead lines with a felt-tipped pen, which gives me the pattern of the pieces of glass I will cut. The width of the felt-tip line is equivalent to the width of the heart of the lead and the glass is cut on each side of this line, which is called the cutline.

Next, on to *the back* of some large plain glass screens I paint the pattern of the cutline, using black emulsion paint, to give the impression of the real leading pattern. These screens then have to be set up in the studio, against the daylight, with the black painted lines on the back surface of the clear glass. Only now can I begin the joyful task of actually starting on the new work.

I paint the pattern of the cutline onto the back of a plain glass screen with black emulsion paint. When this screen is set up in the studio, I fix my cut glass in place with plasticine and can see where the lead will go.

Glass is selected from my glass rack in the studio ready to cut according to the cutlines on my design.

Most of the coloured glass that we stained glass artists use is hand-made mouth-blown glass and is coloured all the way through. This is called 'pot metal'. But some colours are also made as 'flashed'. The sheet of glass appears to be solid colour but in fact the colour is merely a skin on one side of the glass while the main thickness of the sheet is clear. This skin or 'flash' can be removed by using hydrofluoric acid, which has to be treated with great care as it is highly corrosive.

So, selecting the glass from my glass racks I can cut the pieces of glass according to my cutline. I have a cutting bench with the top made from quarter-plate glass. There is a light under this which enables me to see through any dark-coloured glass I may be using. Each piece is then applied to the clear glass screens with the artificial lead lines painted onto them, using plasticine.

When all the glass is cut the next stage is to start on the acid-etching. I will have already worked out which pieces require aciding at the design stage. With careful planning you can achieve varying depths of red (or blue, or whatever flashed coloured glass you are using). You mask the darkest areas of colour that you wish to retain, using either a bitumastic paint or a transparent sticky-backed plastic, such as Fablon, as a resist, then mask the entire reverse side of the piece of glass as well to protect it from the acid.

This panel is an example of acid-etched flashed glass.

These are examples of first and second paintings.

All the pieces of glass have been cut and I am pointing out the ones that have been acid-etched.

I immerse the glass in the acid (diluted to the correct strength), leaving it there until the colour has become as pale as I want. For the second, paler hue which I have planned, I carefully remove the glass from the acid, washing and drying it, and then cover the next chosen areas with more of the resist. Back it goes into the acid bath, and so on, until I have maybe four different shades of, say, blue, on one piece of glass, right down to clear white.

When the aciding is completed it is now time to apply the first painting. As I said earlier, the aim of the designer is to control the amount of light coming through the glass so that the viewer looks *at* the window rather than *through* it.

This is done by the use of a special paint, which is made from metallic oxides, pigment, water, gum and finely ground glass. The first step is to paint any features, lettering and hard black lines onto the surface. Using a light-box these features can be traced from the full-sized enlargement of the design. The painted glass now has to be fired in a kiln. When the pieces become red-hot, at a temperature of approximately 600 degrees Celsius, the ground glass in the paint will melt and fuse with the basic piece, which renders the paint permanent. When I have stuck my fired glass back onto the screens I apply more of the paint, this time in a diluted form so that it becomes a wash of tone. When this is dry I can work into it, scratching out highlights with a sharp stick, creating textures with hog-hair brushes or fingertips or anything I like to employ, and then refire the glass.

Examples of the use of silver stain on various tints of glass.

At this stage there is an extra magical thing that I can do and this is to add a clear yellow to the glass. This yellow stain was first used in the fourteenth century and if you look at early mediaeval windows you will see that in portraying a figure which might have, for instance, a white face and yellow hair, there will be a lead separating the white from the yellow. After the invention of the stain, which is made from silver nitrate, you will see figures where the white face, yellow hair and yellow halo will be all on the same piece of glass. It also meant that if you apply this 'silver stain' to pale blue glass you can arrive at varying shades of green. Similarly, you can, if using red (ruby) glass, end up with orange and gold tints. And if this is not enough you can plate these pieces over each other and, yet more magic, you can have all the colours of the rainbow!

(Below) The window I am standing in front of is ready to be made up by the glazier.

(Below right) My glazier Mick Fletcher assembles the glass.

After the cutting, acid-etching, painting and staining (these last two stages maybe needing two or more firings in the kiln) the glass is ready for assembling with strips of lead, soldered at every joint and cemented to make the panel weatherproof. I don't do this part myself, but have a highly skilled glazier to make up my work.

Setting out on my career

My mother had always been very supportive and when I embarked on my three years at the RCA she said that she hoped eventually to have something of mine in her house. After I had received my final Diploma in 1955 she had a hole specially hacked out of the kitchen wall, just the size of a circular panel that I had made at college, featuring harvest-type subjects. Marvellous! I was now an Associate of the Royal College of Art and had a window actually in a building.

This was the first window of mine in a building.
My mother had a hole made in the kitchen wall to
display it after I received my RCA diploma!

Assisting with Coventry Cathedral windows

More important even than that, I was taken on as assistant to Lawrence Lee who, as well as being head of the Stained Glass Department, was also Chief Designer of the ten enormously high windows which were being made for the new Coventry Cathedral. This job was for two days a week. The work was carried out inside the Mural Department of the RCA, which lay within the V&A Museum. The glass walls of this department were high enough for viewing about 30 feet of the nave windows which are approximately 70 feet high. Of course, while working on them we had to be shifting sections around and could never see them in their entirety. But after the first six of them were completed they were exhibited, at their full height, in the immensely high Cast Room in the V&A which normally houses a cast of the Trojan column.

(Above) I am working at the cutting bench; Lawrence is about to stick glass onto the screen, Keith New is working at his bench whilst Geoffrey Clarke is enjoying a cup of tea.

At the same time, Lawrence asked me to assist him in his own studio in New Malden in Surrey where he was doing smaller and more traditional work. This was for one day a week. I had another one-day-a-week job at Hammersmith College of Art and Building, teaching stained glass as a craft to Intermediate level. This I found rather frustrating. Stained glass requires light; teaching stained glass at an evening class in winter wasn't easy. Later, I progressed to a whole day, which was much more satisfactory. I know just how lucky I was to have been in the right place at the right time. Where are the opportunities now for newly-qualified stained glass artists to work on windows 75 feet high one day, and on domestic and small-scale panels the next?

Standing in front of one of the Golden Windows I worked on

St Jerome's Church, Hillingdon

Married now, and living in an apartment in Uxbridge, north-west London, where we had converted one of the bedrooms into a small studio, we needed some extra cash to buy a fridge. I looked for a temporary part-time job to fill my one free weekday. My husband suggested trying the local hospital at Hillingdon, so I bicycled up there and offered my services as a cleaner or something similar. As luck would have it, yes, there was a vacancy in Matron's General Office for about six weeks while one of her staff had a minor operation. So there I was, sorting out nurses' pay and checking postage expenses and other, to me, relatively unimportant things and being thankful that I wasn't permanently in an office job, when Matron's secretary asked, 'And what do you do during the rest of the week?' Amazement registered. The vicar of her local church had just died, and they were thinking of having a memorial window for him. Quick as a flash, I offered to do a design. And I did. Matron was impressed. The design was approved, and in due course the window was made. A small two-light window depicting the Annunciation, with a kneeling Madonna in one light, and the Angel Gabriel in the other, for St Jerome's Church, Dawley, Hillingdon. It was my first church commission. During my remaining week as an office dogsbody, Matron told me that one day there was to be a chapel in the hospital and that maybe I would make a window for it? I was to remember those words…

This Annunciation window at St Jerome's Church, Dawley, Hillingdon was my first church commission. It was the result of a chance encounter when I was doing some part-time work to earn money to buy a fridge.

10

A window for my grandmother

Three years passed. I designed and made heraldic panels for St Mary's Church in Twickenham where my great-grandfather had been vicar. I became pregnant and gave up the teaching job, and working for Lawrence Lee. My grandmother died. At the funeral service in Mapledurham church, one of my aunts whispered, 'Now you must think about her memorial window.'

The first design I produced for my grandmother's window was turned down by the Parochial Church Council. Reason? 'That window,' said their chairman, 'is the one I like to look through while the vicar is giving his sermon.' (!) It meant a complete redesign. This one, for a different aperture, was approved. The window features St Francis and St Cecilia.

With a baby on the way and needing more space, we moved to a detached house a few streets away. We converted a garden shed into a very small studio which made life much easier for the creation of stained glass windows.

The St Cecilia and St Francis window at Mapledurham is a memorial for my grandmother, Caroline Travers.

CECILIA

FRANCIS

Learning a lesson

An enquiry came for a window in Scotland shortly after Joanna was born in 1961. Breast-feeding didn't allow a visit to the site so I took on trust the measurements which my client told me were correct. Apparently I was the second artist she had approached: the first had taken all the relevant measurements and templates of the 10-feet-high window, she assured me, so I could proceed with confidence. My design of a Mother and Child was approved and was passed through the necessary church committees, and I was all set to make a start, but it didn't seem right not to have visited the church.

By now my daughter had progressed to a bottle, so I was free to travel. Up in Scotland, in St John's Episcopal Church in Perth, I looked in vain for a 10-feet-high window. 'It is that one there,' said my client, pointing to a window which was approximately six feet high. The first artist had obviously missed out on measuring the height of the window! Alas, it meant a completely new design. 'It looked so big from where I was standing,' said my client apologetically. There was nothing more that either of us could say, but it was a classic phrase. And a lesson learned. Always visit the site! Another position was chosen – a two-light window in the nave.

In order to carry out this commission I now really needed to have my own kiln. With the birth of Joanna, I wasn't able to travel to Lawrence any more to fire my painted glass, or to use the kiln in the V&A where we fired the Coventry Cathedral glass. The baby's arrival meant the end of my days of going out to work, but it marked the beginning of my career as a practising stained glass artist working from home.

I was given the name of a man who would make a kiln especially for me, any size I required. It was to be run on gas. I explained my situation: new baby, window for a Scottish church (yes, that one).

'How much time to you have between feeds?' asked Mr Luxford.

'About three hours, if I'm lucky,' I replied.

'I'll make you a kiln which will take two hours from lighting up until the final tray, number nine, is fired.'

And so he did. Each tray is relatively small, about 9 inches by 7 inches, but that little kiln, which cost £75 in 1961, is still working hard for me. It was converted from town gas to North Sea gas while we lived in Uxbridge, and when we moved to rural Shropshire it was again converted, this time to running on Calor gas. Only when I was commissioned to make a four-light east window in 1989, did I invest in a large third-hand electric kiln.

Hillingdon Hospital Chapel

While in Hillingdon Hospital's maternity wing for Joanna's birth, I had noticed several paintings on the walls of the day room and along the corridors. Each bore some sort of message of thanks from grateful patients, which gave me the idea of giving one of my panels to the hospital. It was one depicting the Madonna and Christ child, which I had made while at the Royal College of Art. This was gratefully accepted and it was placed in a disused office which was temporarily functioning as the hospital chapel. The real chapel was being built under the new wing of the hospital. I recalled Matron's words...but stained glass was now taking a back seat in my life, as my second daughter arrived four years later in 1965. Once again, I found myself in the maternity wing of the hospital and was told that the new chapel had recently been completed. And had my panel found a place in it, I wondered? No, it had been put away, and was unsuitable since its vertical shape wouldn't fit into the scheme of windows in the new chapel which were all horizontal. This intrigued me, and on visiting the new wing of the hospital and descending to semi-basement level I found the chapel, and understood why my panel wasn't acceptable.

The windows form two long, narrow strips of light which are in fact at ground level when seen from the outside. The concrete walls inside were bare and cold, and looking up at the 13 windows – each about 4 feet wide and 2 feet high – I could see through them the legs of people walking towards the hospital entrance, situated directly overhead. This, I thought, was not conducive to prayer or meditation. Obviously there should be something to make the chapel a personal sanctuary from the outside world. Stained glass? But what a difficult shape: 52 feet long and two feet high, divided by narrow uprights every four feet, giving 13 windows on each side. Some challenge!

Back home, in that freezing November of 1965, with new baby and four-year-old asleep upstairs, the condensation on our metal-framed windows turning to ice (no central heating or double glazing for us in those days), I huddled over the gas fire and embarked on a design scheme for all 26 panels. First came thirteen on the south side. Well, south is not entirely correct as the chapel does not conform to the usual practice of having the altar at the east end. These thirteen windows face east, while the other thirteen face west.

There was another challenge, in that this chapel is inter-denominational, so my design had to include only the most basic tenets of the faith. Having recently been involved in the making of the Coventry Cathedral windows some of the thinking behind their designs had naturally rubbed off on me. So I treated the two long narrow strips of light in the same way. One was the 'God' side, and the other was to be the 'Man' side.

This is the 'God' side of the chapel.
I took my inspiration from the
Revelations of St John the Divine.

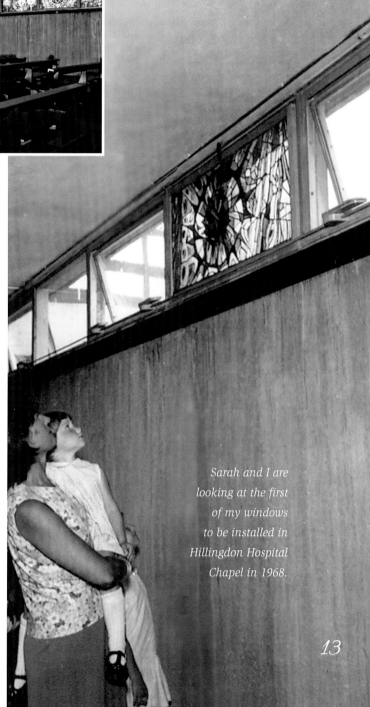

Sarah and I are
looking at the first
of my windows
to be installed in
Hillingdon Hospital
Chapel in 1968.

13

These windows are from the 'Man' side of the Chapel.

On the 'Man' side the story is of Christianity entering the world of man – an ammonite at the centre represents the spark of faith with flanking symbols of the Passion and the Eucharist. Then, continuing outwards in pairs, there are the Hawk and Dove; Integration, and the four Elements of Earth, Air, Fire and Water.

The theme on the 'God' side is taken from the Revelation of St John the Divine, and includes candle flames; spreading evangelizing wings; pearls, jewels and Alpha and Omega.

When I had offered my Mother and Child panel to the maternity wing four years previously, it had been a 'thank you' for the care and attention I had been given. Now I had designed 26 panels without thinking about cost or commissions. Had I been really stupid? I was soon to find out. A meeting was arranged, and I bicycled up (again) to the hospital where the architect was very enthusiastic and said my designs were exactly what his chapel needed. I had cast my bread upon the waters and had been repaid, not in sandwiches, but in the largest commission I had ever received! Coming down to earth it was decided that I would offer one panel from each side as my gift of thanks, and the other twenty-four would be paid for by the hospital authority as, and when, they were made and installed.

My elder daughter was now attending school, and the younger one had started at a playgroup on three weekday mornings. I had arranged a 'baby exchange' with a friend, which gave me one clear working day during the week, plus three short mornings. I never forgot my priorities and was always there when the children came out of school.

The chapel windows were made using an appliqué technique, in which pieces of coloured glass, acid-etched, painted and stained where necessary, were stuck, using a transparent epoxy resin, onto a basic sheet of clear quarter-plate glass. This all had to be done over a light box. When the resin had hardened the spaces in between the shapes of glass were grouted with a black cement, giving the effect of lead lines, which could be varied in thickness by leaving larger or smaller gaps between the coloured pieces of glass. It is a technique suited to contemporary architecture but as yet I think it is unreliable. After some twenty-five years the resin on the sunny side has yellowed badly. I had taken this possibility into account and fortunately my rather abstract designs have not suffered too much from these areas of extra colour.

These windows are from the 'God' side of the Chapel.

The chapel windows were finally completed in 1973. I have always tried to have really good photographs and slides taken of my work and every student should be encouraged to do the same. The Council for the Care of Churches was happy to have some of my slides for their files, as was the Society of Designer Craftsmen, and, later on, I was selected to be on the Slide Index of Craftsmen at the Crafts Council.

The Martindale era

In 1974 the vicar of St Peter's Church in Martindale, Cumbria happened to see an exhibition of work put on by the Society of Designer Craftsmen and was impressed by the excellent standard of work. He had been thinking of having some stained glass in his little Victorian church and wrote to ask if they had any stained glass designers on their books. They did, and he was sent a selection of slides by several of them, including mine. He chose me, as he described my work as 'modern mediaeval' and thought my approach might complement the interior of the church.

One of his parishioners was hoping for a memorial to her husband, a naval officer, who had gone down in the HMS *Glorious* in 1942. It was to be the first stained glass window in the church. At that time, all the windows were glazed with plain diamond quarries, and Charles Barrand was keen to introduce some colour. He sensibly suggested that I should not just do the one, but all five windows on the south side of the nave to give a feeling of continuity, and he trusted that he would find the money to pay for them all. In due course he did.

Between 1974 and 1981 I designed and made fifteen windows for St Peter's Church in Martindale, Cumbria.

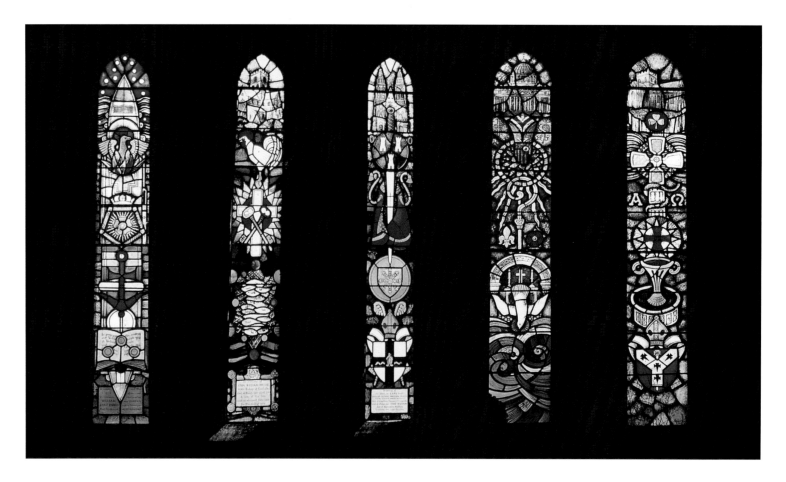

The windows are all single lancets, each 12 inches wide and 6 feet 9 inches high. The vicar had chosen five saints. I said no. Arranging figures within those narrow apertures would result in either long, thin Modigliani-type saints, or tiny figures in the centre of the space with the usual plinth or inscription at the bottom and canopy overhead. 'Not on,' I said. 'But what about using the symbols of the saints?'

This was agreed and with both of us doing research on Saints Nicholas, Peter, Martin, Ninian and Patrick, we became close pen-friends. The scheme was submitted and passed through the PCC and then the Blackburn Diocesan Advisory Committee.

I should mention here that all stained glass windows are made up in sections, since it would be impossible to transport a window six feet high in one piece. Another reason for dividing up the window is that at the time of its installation it will no doubt have to be carried up a ladder by the person who is fixing it in place. When designing

These windows on the north side of St Peter's depict the Nativity, the Passion and the Resurrection.

a window, the artist has to decide where to place these division bars, making sure that they don't cut across important features such as hands or face.

By 1975 the first window was completed, so I packed it – three sections to a window – in shallow crates and took it with me by train to the Lake District. I did this every time another of the lancets was ready.

The vicar used to meet me at Penrith station and then there would be this enchanting drive through the hills and valleys to Martindale, where I would stay at the Vicarage and then supervise the fixing of the latest window on the following day. His wife was a marvellous cook and I really enjoyed these visits.

While I was still working on the fifth and supposedly last window, I had a telephone call from the vicar. He had been given money by some people in America whose name was Martindale to spend on his beloved church, in whatever form he wished. He chose to commission two more windows, this time for the west end of the church where the pair of tall narrow windows each measures 12 feet high by 12 inches wide. He also chose the theme, the Benedicite, which is found in the order of service in Morning Prayer.

Although my first reaction was that the space to be filled (and all design is basically space-filling) would present enormous problems, when I sat down facing that blank sheet of paper on the drawing board the design came relatively easily. The canticle is, in fact, a long list of 'the works of the Lord' and I simply wrote them down in two columns alternating them first left then right, all the way through. I ended up with two lists of words and then put them together into two separate designs which each stand up on their own but also form a satisfactory pair when viewed from some distance away.

The two columns are as follows:

Angels of the Lord	Winds of Heaven
Waters	Night and Day
Fire and Heat	Winter and Summer
Frost and Cold	Seas and Floods
Lightning and Clouds	Things that live in water
Mountains and Hills	All ye Beasts
All ye Green Things	Priests of the Lord
Fowls of the Air	Spirits and Souls
Children of Men	Israel

On the motto ribbon, the words are written in Latin.

This is the first of the two Benedicite windows I designed and made for Martindale church. I chose to interpret the Children of Men by the male and female symbols.

I chose to interpret All ye Green Things by a micro-photograph of a section through a plant cell.

This window is based on the subjects in the second column and I chose to represent All ye Beasts by a mythical unicorn and the Spirits and Souls of the Righteous by haloes.

And it was while I was working on the Benedicite windows that the vicar, 'on cloud nine' as he put it, contacted me again saying that he had just realized that Jubilee Year (1977) was fast approaching and of course there had to be a celebration of this in the form of a window, or windows.

There were three narrow lancets behind the choir stalls, each measuring 4 feet 6 inches by 8 inches wide. Could I please place the full achievement of the Royal Arms here? This would have been impossible, since a 'full achievement' consists not only of the central shield but also the helmet, crest, mantling, supporters and motto ribbon.

You can see here how the various problems were overcome. By rearranging the 'ingredients' I have filled the three lights, even including the blue Garter ribbon which now has different words, but they are words used in the Coronation Service – the 'vivat-vivat-vivat' shouted by the choirboys and the words (in Latin, of course – Charles had a passion for Latin and heraldry) 'Annus Jubilaeus 1977'.

These three little windows were paid for by the local people. Many a coffee morning was held, many a raffle ticket was sold, and trips on the paddle steamer, which is active on Ullswater, helped to fund the project.

This is the window for Charles Barrand, the vicar at Martindale. I have included cymbals, a harp, pipes, a horn and musical notes for St Cecilia and within that small space are some of the flowers which he grew in his vicarage garden.

By now the church was losing its plain glazed windows. Charles was determined to fill them with colour. He asked me to design a scheme for the remaining three windows on the north side. These were for the Nativity, the Passion and the Resurrection. Once again I treated them symbolically rather than naturalistically and donors were forthcoming. One was a widowed lady who wanted a memorial while she was still alive, so the inscription reads 'in sincere appreciation' rather than 'in loving memory'.

Another request was from the owner of the fantastic Sharrow Bay Hotel, situated on the banks of Ullswater. And the third was a group effort, including contributions from Charles himself.

The end of this memorable era came when Charles died in 1981. There just had to be a window for him and, yes, there was one available. Similar to the Jubilee lancets in size, it is in the chancel. He shared his birthday, November 22, with St Cecilia, patron saint of music and his favourite psalm, number 150, praises the Lord in the sounds of musical instruments.

In between my large commissions I often work on smaller secular pieces. The bowl of flowers was exhibited in the British Society of Master Glass Painters Exhibition 'Forty Centimetres Square'.

Diana and John's windows

Somehow I fitted in several other commissions during the 'Martindale era'. We had dear friends in Dorset who had spent a holiday in the Lake District staying at the Sharrow Bay Hotel. They let me know how much they liked the windows in St Peter's and when Diana was killed tragically in 1977, John, her farmer husband, was very keen for me to design and make a memorial for her in their local church in Worth Matravers. It is only a very small window and when it was made I travelled down to help install it. It was a sad and moving occasion and John and I exchanged tears and hugs. Through his tears he asked that when it was his turn, could he have the window directly opposite which was the same size and could it contain the view from their house which looks towards the sea? Of course, I said. It was seven years later that I made his memorial.

This memorial window for Diana Strange centres on the Elizabethan chalice used in the church of St Nicholas in Worth Matravers, Dorset.

John Strange asked if, when the time came to do this window, I could include the view towards the sea which they saw from their farmhouse.

The Chapel inside Warrington Hospital has a very small window of mine. It is a cross in a night sky, one of the simplest of my church windows, and one of my favourites.

O LORD

Thou hast me out and searched known me

PSALM 139

St Bernadette at Uxbridge

Quite close to our home in Uxbridge there was a Roman Catholic church dedicated to St Bernadette. There were two circular windows high up on each side of the sanctuary to be filled. I knew the story of how the Virgin Mary appeared to Bernadette but I didn't feel able to tackle a pair of designs involving figures at such a height. The result was a very abstract couple of windows showing an indication of the Grotto surrounded on the one side by ivy, and on the other by roses, with a stream of water droplets running through the designs.

One each side, within the Grotto, there is a mystic rose representing the appearance of the Blessed Virgin Mary to the young Bernadette.

On the day of the installation of these circular windows in St Bernadette's there was a strong wind blowing. The local man who was fixing the glass lost his balance while he was at the top of the ladder, and, in order to save himself from falling, he leaned heavily against the semicircle which he was about to fit. Alas, although he saved himself, the section of the window was severely damaged, which meant time lost while repairs were carried out by yours truly. I am happy to say that this has been the only time such an accident has occurred during installation of my work.

23

This very simple window at Pishill church is a memorial to my aunt, who had been a doctor. The words of her favourite prayer were worked using acid-etching.

A window for a favourite aunt

In 1985 my favourite aunt lay dying. During her final days, she said that she would like me to make her memorial window in Pishill church, near Henley-on-Thames. All four of her grown-up children suggested themes and subjects relevant to her life that could feature in the design. These included: a view of her house, a cornucopia, medical symbols (she was a doctor), wine-making equipment, a cow, a candle, lines of poetry, and much more besides. The window measured only 3 feet 9 inches by 1 foot. I did produce a design but it was very crammed with far too many things, and eventually I destroyed it, coming up instead with a very simple arrangement using acid-etched lettering of one of her favourite prayers set against a plain background representing the elements. This solution pleased all the family.

Stained glass in houses

It hasn't all been church work. I was asked by an architect friend to design a decorative border for the top half of a door in an extension that he was planning for Lady Rachel Billington's house in London. When I met her to see the proposed site I noticed that she was obviously keen on small and delicate ornaments and trinkets, so I included the initials and names of her two children; her own and her husband's initials; red roses and white lilies (rather classical tokens of love) and the rest of the border was made up with wild flowers, butterflies, bees, wild strawberries and suchlike. She was very pleased with the result.

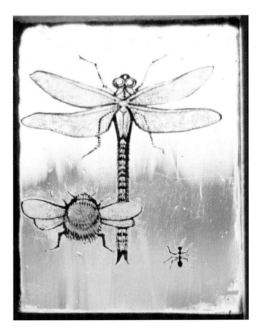

This decorative border
contains many personal
links to the family.

Cambridge Rival

Grandee

Shortly after the job was installed I had a call from her sister, Lady Antonia Fraser, who had particularly loved the wild strawberry. Would I please come and see her to talk about a window in her house? Of course I would and did. As I entered the hall I was instantly aware of … strawberries! On the hall table there was a vase decorated with them; a strawberry-shaped platter to receive keys; a strawberry-shaped pincushion and all up the walls and stairwell the place was papered with them. (And yes, when I eventually used her bathroom, what did I see on the washbasin?) She wanted a border for an arched window halfway up her curved staircase, a lovely setting, which framed a tree growing in her garden. Subject matter: only strawberries, please! Whether or not it had something to do with her surname – Fraser – linking with fraise, the French word for strawberry, I never knew, but she said that because her friends knew of her love of them, she would be given the odd strawberry object if they found one on their travels.

From the technical point of view, I had to divide the border into 35 panes, approximately 4 inches by 5 inches, and use mostly flashed ruby glass, allowing me to place a red strawberry, gold leaves and some lettering in each pane. I thought it might be rather dull just to portray one type of fruit, so I went to the Natural History Museum and found several varieties in different shapes and sizes and, as punctuation, I labelled each one with their correct name. My client was very pleased.

I included and labelled many of the varieties of strawberries I learned about in the Natural History Museum.

Strawberries were to be the main feature of this staircase window.

Other domestic windows

When we were living in Uxbridge and my younger daughter was just a toddler, some of us mums would visit each other's house for coffee. On one of these mornings the lady of the house said how much she liked my work and, if ever she came into any money, she would like to commission some stained glass. Several years later she did in fact become a wealthy woman, and, true to her word, I was invited to design and make a room divider in the form of a glass screen for her new home near Bristol. (How we arrived is another story, but suffice it to say I had never flown in a helicopter before!) Her favourite colour was red, and I filled eight 18-inch square panels with white flower heads etched from ruby glass, surrounded by their foliage. Four years later, she wanted another screen. This time it had to be fruits, portrayed in their natural colours. Quite a challenge.

(Above) This panel of eight squares forms a room divider for a client whose favourite colour was red.

I was asked to produce another screen to include fruits. The challenge was to make the colours look natural.

These anemones were made using flashed glass which has been plated.
The panel forms a fanlight over a front door.

28

Other domestic work I have done include a backstairs window and a fanlight of anemones, their colours being shown correctly using plated red and blue glass; another staircase window featuring the client's favourite flowers; and a front door with two vertical panels of roundels, one on each side of the door, containing different flowers. This was for the owner of Bayley's Garden Centre, near Shrewsbury.

This staircase window featured the owner's favourite flowers.

This detail from panels either side of a front door were made using blue and red glass which were treated with acid, paint and stain then plated to give a wide range of colours.

*This window
featuring Solomon's
Seal was positioned
on a backstairs.*

There was another call from Lady Rachel Billington. Four years had passed since our last meeting and she was now the proud parent of two more children and felt that they too should have some stained glass to commemorate their births. Would I come to see the site for the proposed second panel?

*This door panel,
depicting harvest,
commemorates the birth
of two more children
in the Billington family
and makes a pair with
the door on page 25.*

Fortunately she had another door almost exactly like the first one so, choosing a harvesting theme, I included corn, blackberries, apples, pears, poppies and the like, not forgetting the children's names and initials. 'That's it,' she said. 'I haven't any more doors so I won't be having any more babies!' And then what happened?

Well, Lady Antonia went to tea with her sister to see this new glass. Her circumstances had altered as well. She was now married to the playwright Harold Pinter and thought she would like to give him a 'wedding present' window. Once again I trod the strawberry carpet and then was told of Harold's 'favourite things'. Hers had been strawberries and summer flowers. His was cricket, with his favourite flower being the hollyhock. Somehow, out of this extraordinary mix of ingredients – cricketers, wickets, bats, balls, honeysuckle, roses, hollyhocks, initials, butterflies, garlands, more strawberries and lettering, I concocted a large sash window for her to give to him.

Cricket combined with hollyhocks was the theme of this wedding present window which Lady Antonia Fraser gave to her husband Harold Pinter.

I am standing in the studio by one of the alphabet-of-flowers panels for the Marriage Room in the Civic Centre at Uxbridge.

The Marriage Room at Uxbridge

I have also had opportunities for work in the secular field. One of my favourite schemes was to design and make windows for the 'Marriage Room' in the newly built Civic Centre in Uxbridge. These feature an alphabet of flowers. I used an acid-etching technique, removing some of the skin of colour on red and blue flashed glass giving me paler tints of red or blue on each succeeding dip into the acid, taking the colour away completely in some areas. With the addition of black paint and the use of yellow stain I could, on blue glass, achieve different greens, pure yellow, white and different shades of blue on one piece. On the red glass I could get red, paler red, white, orange and yellow. Each panel was made up of twelve rectangles and the shapes of the flowers and leaves ran over the lead lines. All the plants were named and their initials are in the corners of the panels. The Civic Centre was opened in 1979.

Some of my panels in situ in the Marriage Room.

I also designed and made a large entrance screen for this building. It would be seen on entering the front doors, and also from the other side when stairs would bring the viewer up to the next floor. This was a difficult site as there would be light shining both at and through the glass. It was on a different scale from any of my previous commissions, and I felt at a loss in deciding how to tackle it. Finally I chose to keep everything as simple as possible. There was to be no painting on the glass (the lead lines would provide the drawing). The glass chosen would be mainly of tinted whites, with a smattering of double-sided mirror glass, small areas of silver stained glass and a few random pale colours. All these were for the sweeping shafts which led the eye up from simplified heraldic representations of the towns which are twinned with Uxbridge: Mantes-la-Jolie, Schleswig and Emden. The shafts met and passed through a large seven-pointed star towards the top of the design. The points stand for the seven local boroughs which now make up the London Borough of Hillingdon.

In order to make this enormous entrance screen in the Civic Centre I had to hire the gymnasium of my children's school and spent hours on hands and knees drawing out the shafts so that they were arranged correctly.

St Margaret's, Uxbridge

Then it was back to my queue of waiting vicars and I was commissioned by the local Residents' Society to make a Silver Jubilee window for our local parish church St Margaret's in Uxbridge to commemorate twenty-five years of the Queen's reign. This was the Crown Window and featured a large amount of heraldry including the full achievement of the Royal Arms and heraldic shields and symbols showing how during these years Uxbridge had become integrated within the twenty-eight London boroughs and we were now living in the London Borough of Hillingdon.

Although I was asked to make this window for St Margaret's, Uxbridge to celebrate the Queen's Silver Jubilee in 1977, it was 1980 before the Crown Window was completed because I was fully occupied with the Martindale windows.

My 'garden shed' of a studio was not large enough to accommodate this large three-light window, which presented me with a problem. Fortunately, a few years previously, we had had a proper room made in the loft of our house in Uxbridge so that my husband could run his model trains there, and also he could have a solid desk to write at. A large plain window was incorporated into this loft conversion, and it was ideal for the proposed Jubilee window, being wide enough for the three lights, but of course did not have the required height. All stained glass windows are designed in sections, as I have mentioned earlier. This has a reason: when the window is ready for installation somebody will have to place it into the designated hole in the wall. Nobody could carry a 6-foot-high panel of stained glass up a ladder, so each section of a window must be made in panels not to exceed approximately four feet in height, for a man to carry it comfortably.

So my window was made in 'layers' two at a time. These could be shifted around so that I could get the relationship of the sections arranged correctly. I didn't want to cut any glass inside the house, fearful of damaging flooring or carpets, so all the cutting and acid-etching were done in my studio. The glass was then carried in trays through the house and up the loft ladder, and then assembled on a clear glass screen in front of the loft window. Only then could the painting begin.

It was a long and fiddly job. The complete achievement of the Royal Coat of Arms was in the centre; crowns, and various heraldic and local badges were included. It was finally dedicated by Bishop Gerald Ellison of London on 22 June 1980.

This is Kiril's roundel. My husband was always a great supporter of my work and I wanted to give him something unique and personal. This initial K is made from two pieces of glass plated together, one blue and one red. I have etched them and stained them, but have not used any paint. The black effect is made by placing the small dark blue areas over the darkest areas of red. You can just make out a thin circle of blue around the outside edge. In this roundel I have used not only hydrofluoric acid but also another which is called 'white acid'. This gives the effect of sandblasting.

Secular windows

Another secular window was for Ruislip Library. In 1987 money had been given for 'something to mark the 50th anniversary of the Library' and this coincided with the death of one of the librarians. The staff decided against providing yet another bench in the reading area and chose to commission a window.

Incidentally, this was the first window that I made when we arrived in our new home in Shropshire, and the willow leaves were drawn from trees which grow close to the house.

I placed a 'Tree of Knowledge' against some flowing water, and set a book beneath the tree, with willow leaves in the border. The tree was a pollarded willow. The name of the recently deceased librarian was Miss Pollard. I hope she would have been amused.

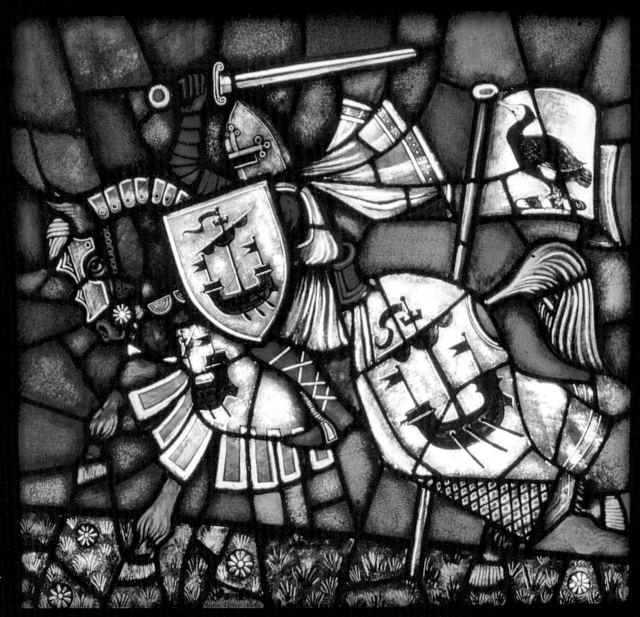

This window was made for an American who bought an Irish castle and wanted a suitable piece of stained glass to reflect his newly acquired status.

Another secular commission was for a castle in Ireland. The client was an American, a Colonel Driscoll, who had bought the castle, changed his name to O'Driscoll and was now finding out through heraldic searches whether there was a coat of arms for O'Driscoll so that he could have them incorporated into colourful stained glass to be set into a wall in his castle. The result of the search was not what he had hoped. The armorial bearings turned out to be a black ship set on a silver background and the crest was 'a Cormorant proper', i.e. its natural colour, which is virtually black. So much for the colourful glass. It was my job to give him what he wanted so I designed a panel featuring a knight clothed in very colourful garb riding a horse which was wearing bright harness and was galloping on a flower-filled field. The shield took second place in this heraldic piece!

In 1983 there was to be an exhibition of stained glass in Southwark Cathedral put on by the British Society of Master Glass Painters. I submitted an alphabet of flower roundels, all acid-etched, painted and stained, using blue flashed glass, arranged in a cabinet. It was this cabinet that led to my being proposed for entry into the Worshipful Company of Glaziers, and I became the first woman stained glass artist in the Company.

There were more heraldic jobs in the form of small panels for Apothecaries' Hall in London, and for Glaziers Hall near London Bridge. The Glaziers share their hall with two other Livery Companies, one being the Launderers, whose Master commissioned me to design and make their Arms, to be placed in the banqueting hall.

This roundel contains the arms of the Worshipful Company of Glaziers.

39

This floral panel was commissioned by wine expert and garden writer Hugh Johnson as a fanlight in the door between his kitchen and conservatory.

Another domestic job that was both very enjoyable and extremely difficult was one I did for the author Hugh Johnson, who has written widely about wine and gardening, and had seen my windows in the Marriage Room and wanted a fanlight over the door leading from his kitchen to his newly built conservatory. Please would I include plants which he grew in his own garden to show the seasons? I designed the panel using the Corsican Hellebore for winter, the Crown Imperial Fritillary for spring, Agapanthus for summer and Japanese Anemones for autumn. At each side of this horizontal panel I placed a vine bearing some delicious-looking green grapes. He was delighted and confessed that he really preferred the subject of wines to that of gardening!

Other church commissions

Meanwhile the commissions for memorial windows were arriving steadily. One of the smallest of these was a tiny window in the porch of a little church in Gatton. Such a sad story. A little boy of about four years old was playing in the churchyard while his mother was inside doing the flowers, and by some cruel stroke of fate a stone cross on one of the graves fell and killed him. When I was met at the station by the farmer and his wife, I was somewhat comforted to see that there was, on the back seat, a carrycot containing a small baby. We went into the church to discuss the placing of the proposed window, and found that the existing windows were all very large and in a heavily painted style. I didn't think my work would look right next to them and suggested putting my window into the porch where its position would enable children to see it at a suitable height.

My brief was to include, if possible, the church at the heart of this agricultural community at Gatton in Surrey. This I did, and I surrounded it with corn, oats, barley, poppies and other plants, and also with bees, butterflies, ladybirds, a caterpillar and a grasshopper. Small roundels containing a calf, a tractor and a combine harvester were set among all these.

41

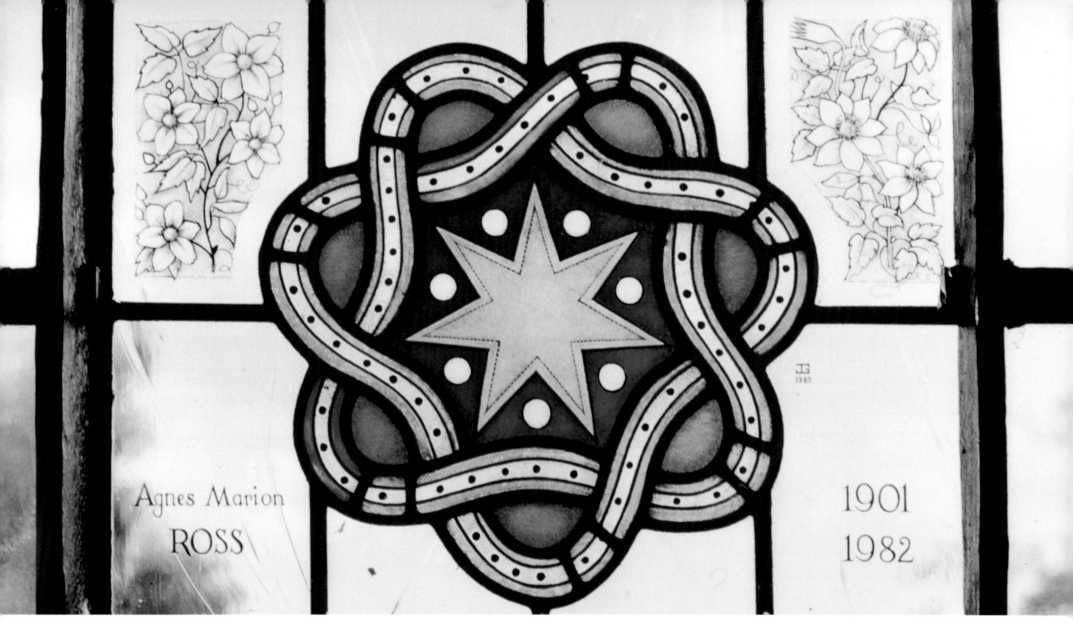

Agnes Marion
ROSS

1901
1982

During the next nine years I designed and made sixteen more church
windows and then, in 1989, two small memorial circular windows in
St Mary's, Twickenham for my parents who had recently died.

A. Denison
ROSS

1902
1985

These two windows are memorials to my parents in St Mary's,
Twickenham.

The next one was to be my largest to date – a four-light east window in Pitminster, near Taunton in Somerset. The existing window was damaged and in need of major repairs. The PCC decided to have a new window rather than restore the old one. My luck (again) was in. They chose me, having found slides of my work in the files of the Central Council for the Care of Churches.

It is difficult to design a four-light window as there is no obvious focal point. After visiting the church and meeting members of the PCC we discussed possible themes and subject matter. The church is dedicated to St Andrew with St Mary. It was felt that this window should contain a strong Christian message and I chose, this time, to include figures. Christ is calling Andrew to follow him. They are both holding fishing nets; while in Andrew's nets there are fish, in the nets held by Jesus there are people. The two central figures stand beside the sea, with the fishing nets turning into shafts framing a heavenly city above.

In this window for St Andrew's Church at Pitminster in Somerset, I chose the theme of Christ calling Andrew to be his disciple.

This window was made in Shropshire. There were several reasons for leaving Uxbridge. My husband had retired by now and wished to be out of a town environment. Uxbridge was becoming noisier as the M25 was nearing completion and we could hear constant traffic noise. Our elder daughter had left home, and the younger one had just been accepted onto a degree course in Stafford.

I was becoming increasingly frustrated at the lack of space in my 'garden shed' of a studio. The most recent commission made in Uxbridge was the huge panel containing the Arms of the Launderers' Company mentioned earlier. It is my usual practice to invite the client to view his or her window while it is still up on the screens in the studio, that is, before the leading is done, as at that stage it is reasonably simple to make any alterations necessary. The client in this case was the Master of the Launderers' Company.

In conversation we mentioned the possibility of moving away from Uxbridge, and he, who happened to live in Staffordshire, suggested that we would find house prices much lower if we went at least 300 miles north of London. After consideration we decided to travel up to Stafford to see our daughter in her new 'digs'; then, heading west, we would call in at estate agents in any of the towns which attracted us, looking for properties which had outbuildings. I needed something to convert into a studio. My husband wanted somewhere to accommodate his 0-gauge model railway track.

We eventually found Ferry Cottage, on the banks of the river Severn just outside Shrewsbury, and it had just what we had hoped for. There was a modern barn which was converted into a studio for me, while the two loose-boxes and a tack room became the 'loco-shed' for my husband's models.

My home at Ferry Cottage provides me with inspiration at times. The idea for the willow tree in the Ruislip library window came from one in the garden.

Soon after we arrived, there was to be an exhibition of ecclesiastical work in Shrewsbury Abbey. I was approached by the vicar who invited me to enter some glass. I explained that, as my work comes from commissions, all I would have to show would be the designs, not the actual glass. That would be fine, he said, and so I arranged some of my recent designs on the table provided. What I didn't know was that the ladies who ran the Abbey gift shop were members of the Guild of St Winefride, and over the years they had been saving the profits from the shop to provide some sort of beautification for the Abbey. When they saw my display they decided to commission a window dedicated to St Winefride. So once again my luck held: the window was installed in 1992. It is quite a large one, six lights on two levels and it is in the north aisle of the Abbey.

Starting with the central light at the top, the Trinity is represented by the Holy Spirit in the form of a dove; God the Father and Creator is shown on the left by a vortex and the Lamb of God, The Son, on the right. This Trinity is linked by a blue ribbon decorated by crosses and drops of water which continues throughout the design and joins the different aspects of St Winefride's faith and work. Her spiritual strength is portrayed by the large red cross with an encircling radiance and a scroll proclaiming 'In God is all my trust'. Small jewels appear in all three lights, and her initial is at the foot of the cross.

In the left light and under the vortex is the corn and on the right are the grapes. Both symbols form a timeless reference to the Eucharist. Below is the ship, symbol of the Ecumenical church throughout the world as used by the World Council of Churches. On the right are seven doves representing the seven gifts of the Holy Spirit: wisdom, counsel, fortitude, knowledge, piety and fear of the Lord. Two small roundels with Alpha and Omega ('I am the Beginning and the End', says the Lord, in the Book of The Revelations of St John the Divine) link the upper and lower levels of the whole window.

In the central light at the lower level St Winefride is set against a starry background holding the Martyr's Palm and Cross. She stands within a richly decorated frame and under a canopy which contains her martyr's crown. The water which is said to have gushed from where her severed head fell is shown issuing from a fountain at her feet and spreading into the adjoining lights.

The Abbey church in which the relics of St Winefride once lay is dedicated to Saints Peter and Paul, founder members of the universal church of Christ. Their symbols are at the top of these lower lights: on the left the crossed key and the inverted cross for Peter; on the right the sword, the book and the anchor of the soul for Paul. Below the crossed keys (in the left light) are the sword of St Winefride's martyrdom; Holywell, the place of pilgrimage; a shield with a cross fleuretty and a chough (heraldic symbols in the County Council arms for Flintshire and Clwyd) and a roundel showing the Welsh poppy; and the heraldic badge of the Principality of Wales. In the lower band of the continuous blue ribbon are the words 'Saint Winefride Martyr'.

The St Winefride window
in Shrewsbury Abbey.

47

St Peter's Church

In 1990, I had a commission for a circular east window for another church in Shrewsbury, St Peter's on Monkmoor Road.

I designed this to include important numbers contained in Christian iconography: three stands for the Trinity (Body, Mind and Spirit), four for the material world of the Elements. Put them together and seven becomes a combination of the worlds of matter and spirit and is thus regarded as the perfect number.

At the centre of the window is the Chi-Ro, or monogram of Christ, placed against the emblems of St Peter: two crossed keys and an inverted Latin cross. Behind this appears a seven-pointed star and seven white shafts of light. Referring to St Peter as a fisherman there are fishing nets or sails suspended from seven points around the circumference, with brightly coloured floats among them. Around the outer edge of the design seven fish swim in a turquoise sea.

Images relating to St Peter the fisherman can be seen in this window for St Peter's, Monkmoor, Shrewsbury.

The window in Fitz church

One of the local 'landed gentlemen' died in 1991 and his widow asked me to design a memorial window for him in Fitz church, which is close to Shrewsbury. She had a strong feeling that he would have liked a Virgin and Child to be included, so these figures form the centre of a large single-arched window in the south wall of the church. I learned of Sir David Offley Wakeman's love of trees and that on his two estates he had planted many of them. Lady Wakeman wondered if I could incorporate some heraldic figures in the form of family crests. She wished for a clear background behind the figures but did not seem to appreciate that the viewer would then see through the clear glass and view the greenery of the shrubs growing outside that wall of the church. I provided some sort of compromise by painting a very faint haze around the figures, forming a little copse to make the outside greenery less noticeable.

The Virgin is standing holding the baby Jesus within an arched border containing leaves from many of the different trees Sir David had planted on his two estates: Yeatton Peverey and Rorrington. They are all named. Placed against this inner border are seven roundels. They depict a large cross; the monogram of Maria; a crescent moon, symbolizing motherhood, and his two estates and two family crests. Small shields in the background contain the symbols of St Peter and St Paul to whom this church is dedicated.

Sir David Offley Wakeman's love of trees and views of his family estates are an important part of the design in his memorial window at St Peter and St Paul's Church at Fitz in Shropshire.

49

Fiftieth anniversary of the D-day Landings

Shortly after this, the Royal British Legion wanted to commemorate the 50th anniversary of the 1944 D-day Landings, and my window, marking this historic event, was dedicated in 1994 in St Mary's Church, Chirk.

The inspiration of the Cross forms a centre for the spiralling shafts representing the work of the Royal British Legion. They pass over and through several perfect circles. The first is red, denoting war and wounding; the second is gold for peace and harmony; the third is multicoloured for other communities, and beneath there is an indication of yet another circle. All these shafts are edged with blue and red, referring to the Union flag. They focus on the symbols of the British Isles – a leek, a rose, a thistle and a shamrock. The badge of the Royal British Legion is at the base of the design, and there is a scattering of poppies in the background. It was dedicated by the Archbishop of Wales on 12 June.

This Royal British Legion window commemorating the 50th anniversary of the D-day Landings is in St Mary's, Chirk.

In contrast to the large window in Chirk, I made a small memorial
window in St Mary's Church, Sullington for their verger, who had
been a carpenter. In the design I have featured the chalice which
is a representation of the one used in their communion service;
lilies for Mary; a collection of carpenters' tools; peacock feathers
(the peacocks, who lived in the Manor House next door, sometimes
joined the church services, said the vicar wryly). There is also a
view of the Sussex Downs, and at the centre is the church key. It
was after opening the church one day and kneeling to pray that
the verger died. His daughter then took over as verger. She is also
remembered in this little window.

This small window at
St Mary's, Sullington
in Sussex is a
memorial to the local
carpenter and verger.

Shrewsbury Abbey

One of my friends wondered why there was no memorial to St Benedict, founder of the Benedictine Order, in Shrewsbury Abbey. He suggested to the vicar that maybe a window to St Benedict might be a welcome addition to this former Benedictine abbey? The result of this was that I received a phone call from the vicar. 'Don't get excited, Jane, but we're thinking of having another window, and while some of us like your St Winefride window there are others who think that we should offer the commission to another artist. Could you, therefore, give me the names and addresses of several stained glass artists you could recommend?'

I did some research, and called him back and, as an afterthought, asked, 'If this is to be a competition, may I enter?'

'Yes,' he said. And I did. And I won. The Benedict window is over the south door of the Abbey, again a three-light window. It was installed in 1997.

But before this I was to have a major upheaval in my life. I had started my first attempts at a design for the St Benedict window in January 1996 and had struggled to find any solution, after two whole days of reading about his life and the Benedictine Order, looking at pictures of the Italian landscape; listening to music; and generally trying to immerse myself in thoughts of the life lived by monks at that time. Designing is the most difficult part of making a window. At last, on 15 January, the first pencil lines started to make sense. I decided to place St Benedict in front of monastery buildings, and to include a vegetable garden where the holy men could grow vegetables and herbs.

The St Benedict window

The figure of St Benedict, founder of the Benedictine Order, is the centre of the design. He holds the book of his Rule, which opens with Ausculta, Fili, Verba Magistri, meaning 'Pay attention, my son, to the words of your Master'; and the combination of prayer and work, to which he attached great importance, is in Latin on a band beneath the book. The saint stands near the historic Abbey of Shrewsbury and close to the distinctive bends of the River Severn. Behind him is a representation of monastery buildings flanked by cypress trees; and at the base his name and dates.

Above the roof is a monogram of Christ, and up in the traceries moon and sun illuminated the gold letters of BENEDICT set against a sparkling night sky. Over everything shines a seven-pointed star symbolizing the fusing of the spiritual (the Trinity) with the physical (the elements of earth, air, fire and water).

At the top of the left-hand light is a roundel devoted to music (a Benedictine monk first originated an academy of music). Early instruments are framed within a five-lined staff with bar lines and musical notations. Below is a monk at work in his scriptorium; a formal garden of herbs and vegetables, each identified; and the Benedictine vows of obedience, stability and conversion of life. The raven and the broken cup in the diamond shape suggest the attempts by dissidents in his own monastery to poison him. Legend has it that the raven saved his life.

Ellis Peters is commemorated in the
Benedict window in Shrewsbury Abbey
for her novels about the fictional
Benedictine monk Brother Cadfael.

Remembering the life and writing of Edith Pargeter (Ellis Peters) 1913-1995

The Gild [sic] of the Freemen of Shrewsbury initiated the concept of dedicating this window to the founder of the Benedictine Order, and in the lower corner is a representation of a Gild member's badge. In the vertical border are the names NURSIA (the saint's birthplace) and ROMA (where he studied).

In the right-hand light, the circle at the top forms a pattern of Celtic knotwork surrounding the opening words of the Benedictine canticle; below that is a monk in the herbalist's chamber; then a second monastery garden with a different variety of plants; a roundel illustrating the hospitality for which the Benedictines are renowned; a pitcher of wine, a goblet, a plate and some bread. In the smaller circle are the arms of Roger de Montgomery on the Holy Cross, used as a symbol of this Abbey church. He founded it in 1083.

In the vertical border SUBIACO and MONTE CASSINO are the names of two monasteries founded by St Benedict. In the diamond shape, author Edith Pargeter (Ellis Peters) of Brother Cadfael fame is remembered by an open book, a quill pen and an inkwell.

During the rest of the month I worked practically every day on the design and finally completed it on 31 January. It passed successfully through the Parochial Church Council meeting, and through the meeting of the Diocesan Advisory Board, although there was a slight delay here. One of the members on the DAC thought I should have been able to depict the herbs without naming them. I wrote back in response and said that I had based my design on an early English herbal, where every herb was named. They accepted, and all the herbs are labelled. I had got the go-ahead on the window, but due to other commissions I couldn't start on St Benedict immediately. Then this life-changing event occurred.

A major upheaval

Life was running smoothly. I had several windows in the pipeline, and was enjoying the fine summer weather and having visits from some of my relatives. There was a social 'do' at the village hall to which I went, and was a given a lift by my near neighbours as my husband didn't wish to attend. There was entertainment to start with: a local choir sang to us. This was followed by a buffet-style meal, where we helped ourselves and then sat at tables to eat. I was sitting next to Justin, the neighbour who had driven me there. Suddenly, I felt a hand on my knee, under the table! I couldn't understand it. Who could be there, and why? I don't know what happened next, but Justin said, rather sharply, 'Jane, are you all right?' I didn't answer. He repeated the question. I found that I couldn't answer. I just sat there. People were getting up to take their dirty plates to the kitchen and to choose a dessert, so in the general upheaval I don't think very many people noticed Justin half-lifting me from my seat and propelling me out of the hall, to stand, holding onto a railing, while he dashed inside to ask the vicar to go and collect my husband from our house.

Unable to speak, I was worried that I'd left a cardigan and a bag at the table. Mercifully, they were picked up by Antoinette his wife, and I found myself with them in their car, heading towards the local hospital. I think that Justin must have phoned the hospital on his mobile, as I was obviously expected.

My right hand was cold and flabby. I felt suicidal. I was put to bed, not knowing what had happened to me. My husband and a dear friend came to see me, but I could say nothing, and they didn't stay long.

I was examined by a young doctor who looked deeply into my eyes with some sort of machine, but I never saw him again. Not only could I not speak, I was unable to use the bedpan, which I desperately needed. My body had obviously gone into shock. Some time later I was very embarrassed to find that I had wet the bed. Everything was out of control! I did sleep. I think I must have been given a sedative.

Next morning, at breakfast, there was a bowl of cornflakes on my hospital tray. I found that my right hand was unable to hold or use a spoon, and had to be helped by my left hand. Only then did I realize that I had suffered a stroke. Luckily I was able to walk, and in the bathroom mirror I noticed that my face looked somewhat twisted. Fortunately this didn't last long.

That first afternoon my husband came to visit, bringing a few necessities, including a biro and a pad to write on. Holding the biro very awkwardly in my right hand I couldn't make any marks…only a shaky dot. It was the worst that could happen. I knew that if I couldn't draw it meant that I would never be able to work at stained glass again. This spelled disaster… Glass had been so important in my life. With my lack of speech I was unable to communicate my deep sadness to my husband. I think he also suffered greatly at this time. By the second day I could actually get some words out; they were mostly incorrect, but I was determined to go on trying and made my own 'speech therapy' by reading aloud, in whispers and very hesitantly, from a book I had been reading. I could hear perfectly well; could understand what was being said, but the stroke had taken away my ability to get any proper words out of my mouth. And this was the same with reading. I could read inside my head, but couldn't get words out, apart from fuddled and idiotic ones.

Naturally, when I arrived home from hospital after my stroke one of the first things I did was to make a small stained glass panel. This is it.

And then my sister came to stay at our house and was allowed to be with me in the hospital. She was wonderful, and stayed three days. I thought that the odd things that came out of my mouth were hilarious, and so did she, so we both giggled our way through those days.

On the second day I had another go at writing, and this time I wrote out the alphabet. All the lower case letters were the right way round and in the correct order! So my brain was still working. But could I draw?

I managed a flower, a very basic one, but it was definitely a flower. Hooray! My spirits soared. The next ten days were spent in hospital, with a gradual improvement in my speech. All stroke patients are required to have a session with a psychiatrist before they leave. In halting words I asked this lady if I would ever completely regain my ability to speak. 'Yes, you should make a good recovery, but it will take at least two years.' She was right. It took about three years, and even now, fourteen years later, I am not 100 per cent word-perfect. Sometimes, in conversation, I make a 'spoonerism' or a hesitation. At first, when I started giving my illustrated talks again, I would tell the audience, and they were always very kind. Nowadays I don't feel the need to rake up the past.

Luckily the stroke had not affected my ability to cut glass, or any other practical part of making a window, and my life was pretty well back to normal. Once more, I felt very lucky. But there was another and more tragic twist of fate. A month after the St Benedict window was installed and dedicated, my husband died. It was completely unexpected. I was comforted by the fact that he hadn't suffered any pain at the end. It had been a massive stroke. But my life had to go on. There were more windows to be made.

(Left) I tried to incorporate many significant features of Ernest Pring's life in his memorial window: his churchwarden's staff, the Boy Scouts and the Bristol landscape.

(Below) This beautiful chalice includes the figures of the apostles. I used turquoise flashed glass and acid etching to recreate it here.

The window in Bristol

In 1997 I was contacted by a retired headmaster (Martin Pring) and his sister, who both lived in Bath. They wanted a memorial window for their father who had been churchwarden emeritus in the Church of the Holy Nativity, Bristol. It is quite a large single light, approximately nine feet tall. I included a view of the church (which can be seen from the train, as it is on the skyline); his churchwarden's staff; symbols of the Scouting movement; his favourite Biblical text; the chalice used in their Communion Service, and primroses to denote his love of wild flowers. A cross dominates the centre of the design and a star beams its light over all.

I attended the dedication of this window, and at some point Martin took me aside and said that when his mother died, would I make a window for her? There was one available just alongside the one for his father. In due course ten years later it came to pass. This time I chose to feature the Virgin and Child with angels, and included roundels showing Martin's mother's activities involving the Church: the Children's Society; the Mothers' Union; Abbeyfield Housing; and the cooking which she did for the Church on its social occasions.

This window is a memorial to Phyllis Pring and is adjacent to her husband Ernest's window at Holy Nativity Church, Knowle in Bristol.

Stanley the model

As I was starting on this design my younger daughter Sarah, married now, produced her first baby son. What better model for the baby Jesus! I had received a photograph of Stanley when he was three days old, and this was perfect. He is now four years old. One day, maybe, he will see himself portrayed in glass.

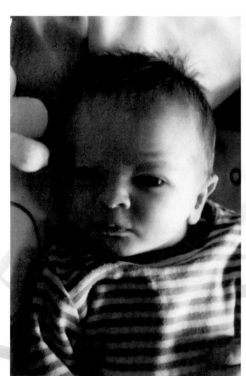

The model for baby Jesus was my new baby grandson Stanley.

Christchurch Priory

Shortly after my husband died I received a request to design a window for Christchurch Priory, near Bournemouth in Dorset. This had to be a window with a 'wow!' factor. The Priory Church Committee commissioning it wanted something to celebrate 900 years of Christian worship on that site. They had already asked another artist to create a design but this had been rejected as the window needed to be non-figurative. So then it was my turn.

The site of the proposed window was in the west wall of the north transept, so it would receive evening light. Remembering my 'brief', I thought I might include a large Cross; spirals; stars; rays of light; bright colours; circles; fireworks; space; music; fire; water and everything weaving over and through each other. The only recognizable symbol would be the monogram of Christ, or Labarum.

This was the first design I had attempted after the death of my husband. He had been the first person to see whatever it was that had been created on my drawing board, and would offer criticism and suggestions that were helpful. This time I had shown my design to no-one. Before sending the design to the church committee, I took it in to a local colour-copying shop to be photographed. There I met the owner of the Shrewsbury Craft Centre, Andrew Wright. He was also waiting for something to be copied. I showed him my design. His reaction: 'Wow!' Had I got it right? Yes! The window was installed in May 1998.

I felt sure that my husband would have liked it and I decided to incorporate some sort of memorial to him in the design. If you ever visit the Priory in daylight, you may be able to make out several little black stars right at the top in the dark-blue area. The little stars have been coated with varnished silver and they should shine out of the background if the lights are on inside. That was my personal offering of thanks to my dear husband.

The window at Christchurch Priory celebrates 900 years of Christian worship on this site.

59

My Fanlight of Flowers was designed and made to go in a recess in the craft centre at the redundant church of St Julian's in Shrewsbury.

Shrewsbury used to have a very interesting craft centre housed in the redundant St Julian's Church. I often visited the centre and enjoyed looking at the various craftsmen and women at work in their individual cubicles and stalls. One day Andrew Wright, who ran it with his wife and actually lived inside the tower of the church, asked if I would like to become a member of this group of exhibitors. It meant being prepared to be in the Craft Centre every Saturday working at my craft in an allotted space and for some days during the week as well.

I felt that I hadn't time to accept his invitation, so instead I offered to make a small exhibition panel of stained glass to be placed in a recess over one of the stone doorways inside the church. Andrew liked the idea and my Fanlight of Flowers was put in place with artificial light to illuminate it. Anyone visiting the centre would see the panel on their way to the main collection of crafts.

Sadly the Craft Centre is no more. The church is open and is now used by different church groups. My panel remains there – it was designed for that particular space and won't fit anywhere else! Andrew is able to see it as he goes towards his home at the top of the tower.

Whitchurch, Shropshire

Another job which entailed quite a lot of research and gave me as much pleasure was a window I did for a house in Whitchurch. The client was a lady who had attended one of my talks (I have, over the years, spoken to many Women's Institute groups, luncheon clubs and the like). She approached me afterwards and told me that her family of husband and two children were all involved in a cheese business and that they were having a new house built. Would I consider making something for this house? Of course! I wrote down her name and address. Years passed and the scheme was apparently forgotten. Not so.

She telephoned me in 2003. The house was ready to receive some stained glass! This was to be in the main reception or dining room, which had a parquet floor, beautiful wood-panelled walls and a huge open fireplace. 'This is where we will have dances,' she told me. Measurements were taken and we all went to the local pub for an excellent meal. Lots of discussion went on as to subject matter and I took notes on the interests and pastimes of each family member. The panel is horizontal, about 4 feet by 2 feet, and is viewed at just above eye level.

This window for a house in Whitchurch reflects not only the town's cheese-making heritage but the family's interests.

At the centre I placed a spiral, representing the churning of the cheese, with the arms of Shropshire County Council, and a tower clock (for which Whitchurch is famous) placed prominently. The borders have an initial at each corner with relevant items by them. Father has some cheeses and a cheese probe; Mother (whom I thought would want flowers) chose to have her hobby included – this is a trout fishing rod plus trout. Son has heraldic badges of his school and Oxford college, along with a symbol of the Conservative party for which he stood in a recent election, and a scattering of old coins which he collects. Daughter has her school badge, with several hobbies portrayed by a thimble, knitting needles, tennis racquets and a kettle. Along the base line I have included a little ginger cat and a West Highland terrier! There is a pattern of oak leaves as well, as the house itself is surrounded by trees. What a mixture! The window was unveiled to a round of applause.

Another local window for a church in Woolstaston is a memorial for Dorothy Bown who was the organist and also the churchwarden. Born in Burma, she had a strong faith, which is shown in the cross and star with its surrounding infinity symbol. I have included several of her interests in the window. She made corn dollies and intricate lace, played the handbells, sat on various committees wielding a gavel and was a keen gardener. At some point Dorothy lived in Kent and also by the seaside, hence the hops and shells.

(Right) Dorothy Bown's memorial window on view in my studio prior to glazing.

(Above) Dorothy Bown owned a black-and-white cat and I was a little worried that the Woolstaston Parochial Church Council might object to seeing a cat included in a church window, but my fears were unfounded.

The Millennium window, St Oswald's, Oswestry

In 2004, one of my 'millennium' windows was dedicated. It is the largest church window I have made so far. Four tall lights, with eight traceries along the top, for St Oswald's Church, Oswestry, Shropshire.

A large capital 'O' fills all four lights. This is for Oswald. Oswestry takes its name from the story of the King of Northumbria who was killed in battle. His enemies cut up his body and nailed some of it to a tree – hence Oswaldstree. At the centre of the large oval is a continuum – symbol of eternity, representing the Faith, with spiralling shafts reaching out to all directions. The tree grows within the remaining space, bearing on its branches roundels which represent fruits, containing signs and symbols connected with the life of Jesus, which is what the Millennium is all about.

The very large Millennium window at St Oswald's Oswestry.

64

(Right) Above the main lights are eight tracery lights. These contain the badges, shields and logos of various clubs, associations, societies and heraldic groups, all connected with the market town of Oswestry. They include Cambrian Railways; Round Table; Royal British Legion; Shropshire County Council; Oswestry Town Council (shown here); Rotary International (shown here); Lions International; Women's Royal Voluntary Service; Orthopaedic Hospital; Royal Artillery; Oswestry Borough Council; Oswald's Cross of Prayer and silver dish; Oswald's crown and the sword which slew him (shown here); the See of Lichfield (shown here); Masons; Oswestry School.

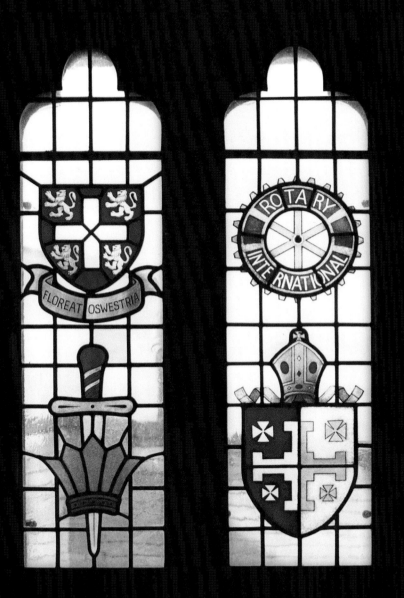

(Above) This small detail is one of six creatures, which appear in the Oswestry window. They reflect the town's agricultural market.

One domestic commission was for a bedroom window in Swan Cottage in Buckinghamshire. It contains a central swan, surrounded by Christmas roses, and the initials of the couple who lived there; all made using ruby flashed glass.

My design for the Wheatsheaf Shopping Centre in Rochdale.

The Wheatsheaf Shopping Centre

The largest secular commission I have ever received was for the Wheatsheaf Shopping Centre in Rochdale. It was for a 30-foot-high window which extends over two floors and portrays the factories and tools of the trade of cotton and woollen textiles. It was far too large for me to make in my studio, so the job of making it was subcontracted to a London firm of stained glass makers. I visited their (huge) studio on a regular basis to oversee progress, and I was very pleased with their work. Sadly, Goddard & Gibbs no longer exists. The enormous window was 'unveiled' in 1990.

67

69

This birthday present for 'a hobbyist' in stained glass also reflects his love of flying aeroplanes.

Other domestic creations of mine include one for a birthday present. The recipient is, to quote his own words, 'a hobbyist' in stained glass. Another of his hobbies is flying his own aeroplane. His wife commissioned me to make a suitable gift for him in glass, to be placed in their home. I knew that he appreciated all the techniques involved in the making of windows as, some time ago, he had attended a local art college as a part-time adult student and learnt the basic skills of cutting, painting and glazing, but acid-etching was not on the curriculum.

We first met by chance in my studio when I had one of my large windows up on show prior to being glazed. He had been invited to come and see it by a mutual friend. He noticed the pieces of glass that had been etched, and said he would really like to learn about acid-etching. Could I teach him? He was a fast learner and was soon creating his own acid-etched pieces. So for his birthday present, I designed something very personal including his own initial (several dips in the acid here), his love of coloured glass and his passion for flying to form a sort of 'windmill'.

Homage to Mackintosh

When I first saw the work of Charles Rennie Mackintosh it took my breath away. Here was a man who had mastered so many skills – his watercolours and flower drawings are exquisite. His designing is endless. There is furniture, stained glass, interiors and all sorts of artefacts. The list seems to continue through all aspects of art and craft. Visiting Glasgow some years ago left a lasting impression, as there were so many things to see.

When I decided to alter the bathroom in our Shropshire cottage in 2001, I asked a neighbour who was a qualified interior designer to make the bathroom into what I call my 'homage to Mackintosh'. The famous motif of the Mackintosh Rose adorns the curtains and the floor; framed prints of his flower drawings hang on the walls; white shelving by the bath contains inserts of small pieces of coloured glass in pinks and purples and the stained glass windows are designed and made by me in the Mackintosh style.

Now in 2010 the work continues. Apart from designing and making windows for churches, I have stained glass in many other venues: secular, civic, domestic, libraries, funeral parlours, to name just a few. I have also made literally hundreds of small commemorative roundels to celebrate birthdays, anniversaries, weddings, memorials and new babies. As I mentioned at the start of this 'memoir' stained glass can be placed anywhere you want to enhance with some beautifully coloured light.

It is difficult to think of a suitable ending to all these words. Stained glass has been a great inspiration in my life and it is the making of it that appeals rather than the appreciation of its history. While I still have my health and strength I will carry on working in the medium I love, be it art or craft.

I hope I have shown that it is a mixture of both of these.

Jane Gray September 2010

All my visitors are encouraged to 'use the bathroom' at Ferry Cottage and enjoy my 'homage to Mackintosh'!

71

STAINED GLASS CHURCH WINDOWS

designed and made by Jane Gray ARCA, FMGP

All dimensions are height by width

1	St Jerome, Judge Heath Lane, Hillingdon, Middlesex. Two-light, north wall. Memorial to Revd J Woollcombe. Annunciation; Gabriel and Mary. 3ft 5in by 1ft 6in	1960
2	Mapledurham Parish Church, Berkshire. Two-light, west wall. Memorial to Caroline Travers. Sts Cecilia and Francis. Each 6ft by 1ft 6in	1961
3	Framfield Parish Church, Uckfield, Sussex. Two-light, south wall behind font. Jesus with children. Each 6ft 3in by 1ft 9in	1961
4	St John, Perth, Scotland.	
a)	Two-light, south wall. Memorial to Rosemary Anstice. Madonna and baby Jesus; angels.	1964
b)	Two-light, south wall. Memorial to Canon Derrick Large. Sts Patrick and Columba. All four lights 5ft by 1ft 6in	1967

5	St Mary, Twickenham. Six small heraldic shields in plain glazing.	
a)	North wall: Arms of King Edward III; Abbey of St Valery; Sir Godfrey Kneller; Sir William Berkeley.	1960–4
b)	South wall: Arms of King Henry V; Walter of St Valery, William of Wykeham. Each 2ft by 1ft 6in	
6	St Clement, Ilford, Essex. Three small windows. King, Warrior, Shepherd, David. Each 3ft 6ins by 11in	1965
7	Hillingdon Hospital Chapel, Middlesex. Interdenominational. Twenty-six panels, all 4ft by 2ft. Appliqué technique (epoxy resin).	
a)	Thirteen on north side: Christ entering the World of Man; the Spark of Faith; Hawk and Dove; Integration; Crown of Thorns; Eucharist; the Four Elements.	1968–73
b)	Thirteen on south side: the Revelation of St John the Divine; the Word of God spreading outwards from Alpha to Omega.	
8	St Michael and All Angels, Verwood, Dorset. Two lights, east wall. Memorial to Lorna Limpus. Madonna with children and birds. Each 2ft 6ins by 1ft 2in	1971

9   St Peter, Martindale, Cumbria (overlooking Ullswater).

Fifteen out of a total of sixteen windows (every window except the east) including small panel of lettering in porch.

a)   Five on south side: Sts Nicholas, Peter, Martin, Ninian and Patrick, with heraldry and relevant attributes.

Each 6ft 9in by 1ft

b)   Three on north side: Nativity, Passion, Glory.

Each 6ft 9in by 1ft

c)   Two in west wall: Benedicite.

12ft by 1ft

1974–81

d)   Three in north choir: Jubilee theme with Royal Arms; Lion and Unicorn; symbols of British Isles.

4ft by 9in

e)   One in south chancel: memorial to Charles Barrand, the vicar who wanted his church filled with coloured light.

Dedicated to St Cecilia; based on Psalm 150; musical instruments, flowers.

4ft 9in by 8in

10   St Bernadette, Long Lane, Uxbridge, Middlesex.

Two circular windows on each side of the sanctuary.

Abstract jewel-like design.

Each 3ft 9in diameter

1975

11   St John the Baptist, Cove, Farnborough, Hants.

North wall. Memorial to the Watts family.

St John and the Diocesan arms.

6ft by 1ft 10in

1977

12	St Mary Magdalene, Wargrave, Berkshire.	
	Two panels, west window, south aisle.	
	Memorial to Ada Maude and Irvin Giles Rankin.	1978
	Resurrection themes; Pomegranates, Phoenix.	
	Budget restricted design.	
	Each 11in by 1ft 7in	

13	St Anne, Great Eccleston, Lancashire.	
	South wall. Memorial to Frank and Beryl Clegg.	1979
	Christ healing lame man; loaves and fishes, multitudes.	
	7ft by 2ft 6in	

14	St John the Baptist, Tunstall, Lancashire.	
	Two lights, south wall. Memorial to Alice Lewis Bridges.	
	Heraldry, symbols/emblems relating to the church and the donor's (Harold Bridges) life and	1979
	work.	
	6ft 1in by 1ft 6in	

15	St Nicholas, Worth Matravers, Dorset. A pair:	
a)	North wall. Memorial to Diana Strange.	1979
	Centres round Elizabethan chalice used in the church.	
	3ft by 10in	
b)	South wall. Memorial to her husband John Strange.	1986
	Suspended cross, corn and grapes, local landscape.	

16   Parish church of St Margaret, Uxbridge, Middlesex.

The Crown window. Three lights over south door. Commemorating 25 years of the Queen's reign.

Shows the complete achievement of the Royal Arms, with heraldic and other symbols of St Margaret and the Boroughs of Uxbridge and Hillingdon.   1980

Commissioned by local Residents' Association and friends of the town.

Each 6ft 6in by 2ft

17   St Andrew, Gatton, Merstham, Surrey.

Porch window. Memorial to farmer Maiklem's small son.

The church itself is central to the design which includes a wreath of corn, oats and barley, poppies and farm machinery, animals and insects.   1980

3ft by 1ft 6in

18   St John the Evangelist, Read-in-Whalley, Lancashire (see 36).

Two lights in south wall. Memorial to Canon Schofield.

Symbols and heraldry relating to the church and his life's work.   1981

Each 6ft 10in by 1ft 10in

19   St Ambrose, Leyland, Lancashire.

a)   North wall. Memorial to Fred Wadge.

Symbols of St Ambrose.   1982

4ft 6in by 1ft 8in

b)   Two-light, west wall.

Benedicite theme.   1986

Each 7ft by 2ft; 3ft circle above

20	All Saints, Chorley, Lancashire.	
a)	West end over font. Memorial to Fred Ollerton.	1983
	The Elements, the Spark of Faith, Dove descending, Alpha and Omega.	
	10ft by 1ft 2in	
b)	Memorial to Gladys Ollerton.	1991
	Nativity symbols.	
	Two panels 2ft by 2ft	
21	St Mary, Harmondsworth, Middlesex.	
	North Wall. Memorial to Agnes Florence Mercer.	
	Cross, wreath of flowers.	1983
	4ft by 1ft 3in	
22	Warrington Hospital Chapel, Lancashire.	
	Simple design of Cross suspended between land and sky, with lettering. Artificially lit.	1984
	2ft 11in by 1ft 9in	
23	St Mary, Penwortham, Lancashire.	
	Two-light with tracery, north wall. Memorial to Ida and Walter Valentine.	
	Symbols on quarry background relating to their service to the church.	1984
	Each 4ft by 1ft 6in	
24	United Reform Church, Ongar, Essex.	
	Over north entrance door. Celebration of the life's work of organist Miss Korf.	
	Scroll with lettering and flowers using blue flashed glass with etching.	1984
	1ft 1in by 4ft 6in	

25   St Mary the Virgin, Ebony, Tenterden, Kent.
        Two-light, south wall. Armstrong family memorial.   1984
        Annunciation, Gabriel and Mary, figures on plain quarry background.
        Each 6ft by 1ft 6in

26   St John the Baptist, Broughton, Lancashire.
        South wall. Memorial to the Houghton family.
        Baptism of Christ by St John. Music, flowers, harvest, birds, insects, choristers, schoolchildren,   1985
        the church itself.
        7ft by 2ft 9in

27   Pishill Church, Henley-on-Thames, Oxon.
        North wall. Memorial to Dr Barbara Pirquet (née Travers).
        Simple theme of the Cross and the Elements, with the complete hymn 'God be in my head' in   1985
        white acid.
        3ft 7in by 1ft

28   Holy Trinity, Colne, Lancashire.
        North wall. Memorial to Thomas Fowler.
        Trinity symbols, Three fishes, processional Cross, with Latin version of St John 1:1; carnations   1986
        and steering wheel.
        6ft by 2ft

29   St Barnabas, Kidderminster, Worcestershire.
        Two-light, south wall. Memorial to Lily and Walter Greaves.
        Symbols of the life of St Barnabas. Buildings, wreath of flowers; trefoil above.   1987
        Each 5ft 4in by 2ft

30	All Saints, Brightlingsea, Essex.	
	Medallions in plain glazed background. Cinque Port seal of Sandwich; lettering; Arms of the Diocese of Lincoln.	1987

31	All Saints, Lightwater, Surrey.	
a)	South wall. Memorial to George Leslie Soan. Background Cross, symbols, flowers. 6ft by 1ft 6in	1988
b)	North wall. Memorial to organist Catherine Challen. St Cecilia symbols. 6ft by 1ft 6in	1991

32	St Peter, Chorley, Lancashire.	
	Two-light, south wall. For Mothers' Union. Symbols, panel of lettering. Each 5ft by 1ft 3in	1988

33	St Margaret, Downham, Billericay.	
	North wall. Memorial to Kathleen and Reginald Prebble. Symbol of St Margaret, red Cross on quarry background. 5ft 6in by 2ft	1988

34	St Andrew and St Mary, Pitminster, Somerset.	
	Four-light east window. 'The calling of Andrew'. Sea of Galilee, boats, nets, fish, heavenly city. 15ft by 7ft 6in	1989

35	St Mary, Twickenham, Middlesex.	
	North and south walls above gallery. Two memorials to Agnes Marian and Archibald Denison Ross (my parents).	1989
	Each 2ft by 1ft 6in	

36	St John the Evangelist, Read-in-Walley, Lancashire (see 18).	
	Two-light, north wall. Memorials to Alan Robert Hutchinson and Arthur Frankland. References to Whalley Abbey, diocesan heraldry, church symbolism.	1989
	Each 6ft 10in by 1ft 10in	

37	All Saints Garrison Church, Dortmund, Germany.	
	Ram's head with motto ribbon.	1989
	4ft 6in by 2ft	

38	St James, Weddington, Nuneaton, Warwickshire.	
	Two-light, south wall. Memorial to Margaret Taylor. Heraldic symbols of Sts James and Margaret; flowers.	1990
	Each 6ft by 1ft 6in	

39	Christchurch, Charnock Richard, Chorley, Lancashire.	
	South nave, centre one of three-light window. Memorial to Albert and Edith Corless. Heraldic symbols, Mothers' Union badge, flowers; on plain quarry background.	1990
	7ft 6in by 1ft 6in	

40	St John the Evangelist, Accrington, Lancashire.	
	North wall in the Pals Battalion (1914–18 war) chapel. Memorial to Robert Hanson. St Mark with winged lion.	1990
	6ft by 2ft	

41   Shrewsbury Abbey, Shropshire.
Six-light (three on three), north wall. Dedicated to St Winefride.
Figure of the Saint; canopy, symbols of Sts Peter and Paul; the Cross; Eucharist; Trinity,   1992
symbols of Wales.
Each 7ft by 2ft

42   St Peter, Monkmoor, Shrewsbury, Shropshire.
Circular east window.
St Peter; nets, floats, fishes.   1992
3ft 8in diameter

43   All Saints, Writtle, Essex.
Two-light east window in the Nicholas Chapel.
Arms of Baroness Platt of Writtle linked with those of Guglielmo Marconi. Phoenix. Three   1992
fishes of Trinity, sound wave symbols.
Each 6ft by 1ft 6in

44   St Paul, Warwick.
Two lights, north wall, on each side of existing window.
Medallion style; symbols of Sts Mark and Paul; Cross and Anchor; Warwick's Castle and   1992
racecourse; Arms of Warwick and the Diocese of Coventry.
Each 11ft by 2ft

45   All Saints, Tunworth, Hampshire.
Four-light, south wall. Memorial to Hon. Julian Berry OBE, DL, JP, Colonel of the Royal Horse
Guards (The Blues).   1992
Items of ceremonial cavalry dress; Army service; ancestry.
Each 4ft by 1ft 2in

46   St Catherine, Penrith, Cumbria.
Two-light, east end, north aisle. Memorial to Joseph Chad Harrison. Symbols of Sts Chad and Joseph; heraldry and relevant attributes.
Each 4ft 7in by 1ft 4in

1992

47   St Peter and St Paul, Fitz, Shrewsbury.
South wall over font. Memorial to Sir Offley David Wakeman.
Virgin and child within border of various leaves, all named. Views of family's country estate; symbols of Mary; Moon and Monogram; family crests.
6ft 5in by 3ft 8in

1992

48   St Mary, Sullington, Sussex.
South wall, west end. Memorial to William Puttick, local carpenter and verger, and his three daughters.
Symbols of Virgin Mary; Monogram and Lilies; Chalice and Host; carpenter's tools; views of Sussex Downs.
6ft 1in by 1ft 4in

1992

49   St John the Divine, Sandylands, Morecambe.
Three-light, south wall. Memorial to the Revd David George Pratt and wife Gwenfron.
Central cross, heraldic references to their lives.
Each 4ft 3in by 1ft 3in

1993

50	St Mary, Chirk, Clwyd.	
	Three-light, north wall. Commissioned by the Royal British Legion.	
	Cross at centre of large spiral; poppies; symbols of British Isles; commemorative lettering and BL badge.	1994
	Dedicated 50 years after D-day.	
	Each 8ft 6in by 2ft	

51	St Andrew, Walton-on-Thames.	
	Arched porch window over south door.	
	Red cross with St Andrew's cross. Alpha and Omega.	1994
	5ft by 6ft	

52	St Andrew, Walton-on-Thames.	
	Internal artificially lit panel in alcove. Memorial to Richard McCullough. Scottish landscape with Eildon Hills.	1994
	3ft 2in by 2ft	

53	St Chad, Slindon, Staffordshire.	
	Two-light, south wall. Memorial for Norman John Simpson and wife Muriel.	
	Symbols relating to lifelong association with farming. The church; haywain; tractor; daffodils.	1994
	Each 4ft by 1ft 4in	

54	St Giles, Badger, Shropshire.	
	Single-light with trefoil above. West wall. Memorial to Dr Margaret Ruth Dix and her father Revd Archibald Dix.	
	The Elements, logo of the National Hospital for Neurology and Neurosurgery. Line of poetry, favourite cat, detail of inner ear.	1994
	Main light 6ft 2in by 1ft 9in	

55   St Peter and St John the Baptist, Wivelsfield, Sussex.

Single-light, north wall. Memorial to Sir Bryant Godman Irvine, former Deputy Speaker of the House of Commons, and to his wife.

Farmland, cattle, Chalice and Host, corn, fruit, flowers, birds. Family crests of husband and wife.

5ft 2in by 1ft 5in

1995

56   St Thomas, Walton-on-the Hill, Staffordshire.

a)   Single-light, north wall. Memorial to Peter, a young airman.

Lancaster bomber caught in searchlights; RAF badge, wreath of flowers, book, Chalice and Host, monogram of Peter.

b)   Single light, south wall. Dedicated to St James.

Scallop shells, Chi-Ro Pastoral Staff; Staffordshire Knot; Grapes and Corn symbolizing the Eucharist.

Each 6ft 3in by 1ft 1in

1995

57   St Wilfrid, Ribchester, Lancashire.

Single-light, north wall. Memorial to Jean Woolley.

Alpha and Omega, the Elements, breaking wave, grapes, flowers, inscription.

7ft 9in by 1ft 2in

1996

58   Shrewsbury Abbey, Shropshire.

Three-light, over south door. Dedicated to St Benedict.

Figure of Saint; monastery; herb garden; symbols of Benedictine Order; memorial to Edith Pargeter.

Each 9ft by 2ft

1997

59   St Ambrose, Leyland, Lancashire.
North wall.
Cross; symbols; landscape.   1997
Given by Mollie Bennett as a thanksgiving.
4ft 6in by 1ft 8in

60   Church of the Holy Nativity, Bristol.
North wall. Memorial to Frank Ernest Pring.
Red Cross; Bristol landscape; motto ribbon; symbols of Boy Scouts; Communion Cup;   1998
Churchwarden's Staff; Star with issuing rays.
9ft by 3ft 4in

61   Christchurch Priory, Dorset.
Single-light. West wall in North transept. Celebration of 900 years of Christian worship on this
site.
Central cross in a starry sky. Non-figurative. Contains elements of space and time and using   1999
colours as in a firework display.
8ft by 3ft 3in

62   St Peter's, Salesbury, Lancashire.
Three-light, north wall. Memorial to Jean Bradley.
Central purple Cross, surrounded by a Circle containing motifs relevant to her life. At the   1999
centre is the Basilica of St Francis of Assisi.
Each 5ft by 1ft 6in

63   St Leonard, Stagsden, Bedfordshire.
Two-light, north wall. Memorial window for Mr and Mrs Bonnett.
Christian signs and symbols.
Each 6ft by 1ft 3in

2000

64   St Margaret, Downham, Billericay.
East window. Theme of Pentecost coupled with celebration of the completion of repairs to
burnt-out church.
12ft by 7ft

2000

65   St Peter, Cound, Shropshire.
Two-light, south wall. To celebrate the Millennium and Baptism.
Includes Cound bridge; Doves of Baptism; Christian symbols.
Each 4ft 6in by 1ft 5in

2000

66   St Sarkis Armenian Church, Kensington, London.
Single-light, north wall over door. Celebrating 700 years of conversion to Christianity.
Armenian Cross, Peacocks of Immortality, Mount Ararat and portrait of the Mother Church.
5ft by 2ft

2000

67   Christchurch, Oxon, Shrewsbury, Shropshire.
Single-light, east end high above the chancel.
Millennium window with Star of Bethlehem, land, sea and date MM.
3ft 3in by 1ft

2001

68	St Mary, Longnor, Shrewsbury. Two oval tracery lights, over east window. Grapes with corn, and Dove with Oak twig. Each 1ft 9in by 2ft	2001
69	St Lawrence, Weston under Penyard, Hereford. Two-light, north side of chancel. Millennium theme, with medallions containing symbols of the life of Jesus. Each 6ft 6in by 1ft 2in	2001
70	St George, Frankwell, Shrewsbury, Shropshire. Window in upper room of re-ordered church. Phoenix overpowering Dragon, with detailed roundels forming a border all round. 9ft by 5ft	2001
71	St Nicholas, Blakeney, Norfolk. Two two-light windows in church porch with tracery lights.	
a)	Faces east. Memorial to Bertie Wootten, Spitfire pilot. Symbols relating to his life in the RAF.	2002
b)	Faces west. Millennium theme. Local groups represented by shields, badges and logos connected by blue ribbon. Each 5ft (including traceries) by 1ft 2in	2002

72   St Nicholas, Wasing, near Aldermaston, Berkshire.
Centre light of three-light window in north wall. Memorial to William and Nance Mount.
Medallions set against plain quarries, featuring the Elements and the Seasons.
Each 5ft by 1ft 5in

2002

73   St Michael, Woolstaston, Shropshire.
Single-light, north side. Memorial to Dorothy Bown, organist and churchwarden.
Christian symbols and subjects relating to her life and work, with favourite cat at the base of
the design.
3ft by 9in

2003

74   St Oswald, Oswestry, Shropshire (Part One).
Millennium window.
Eight tracery lights form the first part of the commission, which contain symbols relating to
Oswestry including civic emblems and logos; heraldic Badges and Shields; several references to
Oswald, Saint and King.
Each 3ft by 10in

2003

75   St John the Baptist, Preen Manor, Church Preen, Shropshire.
Single-light, south wall. Memorial to Philip Trevor-Jones.
Christian symbols and subjects relating to his life and work.
6ft by 1ft 1in

2004

76   St Oswald, Oswestry, Shropshire (Part Two).
      Millennium window.
      Four lights, north wall.
      A large decorative capital 'O'. Within it the Tree of Life, or Oswald's Tree, bears fruits in the
      form of roundels each containing a symbol pertaining to the life of Christ: Nativity Star;   2004
      Crescent Moon with Star for Birth; Lamb of God; Holy Bible; Pelican in her Piety; the Eucharist
      shown as Grapes and Corn; Christian symbol of the Fish, with the Chi-Ro; Pomegranate for
      Resurrection and Eternity, and the Dove for the Holy Spirit.
      Each 6ft 6in by 2ft

77   St Petroc, Inwardleigh, Okehampton, Devon.
      Millennium window.
      Three lights, north wall.   2005
      Celtic cross against a landscape with roundels showing the Grapes and Corn of Eucharist; wild
      flowers, and two stories relating to the life of St Petroc.
      Each 6ft by 14in

78   St John the Evangelist, Pool Quay, Welshpool, Powys.
      Circular window in interior memorial screen.
      Eight lights containing attributes of St John and other Christian symbols.   2005
      5ft 7in diameter

79   Church of the Holy Nativity, Knowle, Bristol.
      North wall. Memorial to Phyllis May Pring, complementing adjacent memorial window for
      Frank E Pring (see 60).
      Virgin Mary with Christ child within a crescent Moon, with Angels; Bristol landscape inside a   2006
      cross; small oval shapes containing logos of the Children's Society; Mothers' Union; Abbeyfield
      Housing, and cooking.
      9ft by 3ft 4in

80 Christ Church, Bicton Heath, Oxon, Shrewsbury, Shropshire.
Single lancet in north wall celebrating 150 years since the building of this church.
Nativity Star; Cross surrounded by Lilies; Dove surrounded by Roses; Grapes within a wreath   2007
of Poppies and Lavender; a Stook of Corn inside a wreath of Christmas Roses.
5ft 2in by 1ft

81 Roman Catholic Church, 'Our Lady, Help of Christians ', Oswestry, Shropshire.
a) Single-light memorial window. One of five lights in west wall.
Standing figure of Virgin Mary set against the sea with a panel beneath her containing symbols   2008
relating to her.
4ft 8in by 1ft 4in
b) Single-light window. One of five lights in west wall.
Standing figure of St Oswald, to the right of central light. He is set against the sea with a raven   2009
at his feet and a panel beneath him containing symbols relating to his life; his prayer before
going into battle.
4ft 8in by 1ft 4in

82 Pradoe Church, West Felton, Shropshire.
Single-light window in north wall. Memorial to Colonel John F Kenyon.
Oak tree against a swirling sky and agricultural land; Bands of Acorns and Oak Leaves; three   2010
small roundels.
5ft 6in by 1ft 3in